Eye Winker
Tom Tinker
Chin Chopper

Eye Winker
Tom Tinker
Chin Chopper

Fifty Musical Fingerplays

Tom Glazer

illustrated by Ron Himler

A Zephyr Book

Doubleday & Company, Inc., Garden City, New York

ACKNOWLEDGMENTS AND CREDITS

Piano Arrangements by T. G. and others

The following titles are all copyrights of Songs Music, Inc., Scarborough, N.Y. 10510, and are reprinted by permission: "The Barnyard Song," "The Bear Went Over the Mountain," "Bingo," "Brother, Come and Dance With Me," "The Bus Song," "Charlie Over the Water," "Come On and Join Into the Game," "The Dicky-Bird Song," "Down by the Station," "Eentsy, Weentsy Spider," "Eye Winker," "Five Little Ducks," "Go In and Out the Window," "Grandma's Spectacles," "Here Is the Church," "He's Got the Whole World in His Hands," "Hush, Little Baby," "I Know an Old Lady," "Jack-O'-Lantern," "I'm a Little Tea-Pot," "Jack and Jill," "Jennie Jenkins," "The More We Are Together," "The Mulberry Bush," "Old Macdonald," "On Top of Spaghetti," "Pat-a-Cake," "Peter Hammers," "Pick a Bale of Cotton," "Pop Goes the Weasel," "Sailing at High Tide," "Shoemaker, Shoemaker," "The Tailor and the Mouse," "Ten Fingers," "Ten Little Indians," "There's a Hole in the Bottom of the Sea," "There Was a Little Turtle," "This Little Pig," "This Old Man," "This Train," "What Will We Do With the Baby-O?," "When I Was a Shoemaker," "Where Is Thumbkin?," "Where, Oh Where?"

• • •

"I Roll the Ball," by Ray Abrashkin, © 1950, Copyright assigned to Soremy Music Corp., New York, 1971. By Permission.

"Little Arabella Miller," by Anne Elliott, © Publishing Services Partnership, Yarmouth England. By Permission. Music by Tom Glazer, © Songs Music, Inc. By Permission.

"The Little White Duck," by Walt Barrows and Bernard Zaretsky, © 1950, General Music Publishing Co. By Permission.

"The Musicians," by Tom Glazer and Charles Green, © 1951, Leeds Music, Inc.

"Put Your Finger in the Air," by Woody Guthrie, © 1954, Folkways Music. By Permission.

"There Was a Little Turtle," words, Vachel Lindsay; music, Tom Glazer, words © 1920, The Macmillan Company; music © 1972, Songs Music, Inc. By Permission.

ISBN: 0-385-08200-2 Trade
      0-385-09453-1 Prebound
Library of Congress Catalog Number 72-97497
Copyright © 1973 by Tom Glazer
All Rights Reserved.
Printed in United States of America

9 8 7 6 5 4 3

AUTHOR'S INTRODUCTION

I came to fingerplays not as an educator, but through the back door, the stage door, in fact, as a folksinger who sang for children a great deal. It became apparent, quite early in the game, that children were intensely delighted in participating in my concerts right in their seats, not only by singing along, for this was commonplace enough, but by acting out songs in various ways. I took advantage of this, as I have mentioned elsewhere, in raw self-defense, in order to retain the child's mercurial attention-span. The better the devices I made up toward this end, the more riveting the attention, and the more the child was pleased. It became quite clear that almost all healthy children have a deep need for dramatic expression, even on primitive levels, which requires the merest encouragement to come out.

Later on I began to realize that the pleasure in this dramatico-musical expression was so great that learning itself was stimulated. Friedrich Froebel, the Father of the Kindergarten (1782-1852) said a long time ago, "What the child imitates he (she) begins to understand. Let him represent the flying of birds and he enters partially into the life of the birds. Let him imitate the rapid motion of fishes in the water and his sympathy with fishes is quickened . . . In one word let him reflect in his play the varied aspects of life and his thoughts will begin to grapple with their significance."

My professional and personal interest in folk music and folklore and in children did not prepare me for the very pleasant shock I received when, in doing research for this book, I learned that Froebel had "collected" fingerplays and children's games in the field as folklorists do, that is, working in the countryside with peasant mothers and their young children. It was this work which gave Froebel the idea of learning through play, which was the foundation of the kindergarten-nursery school movement.

One of the books I looked into was Emilie Poulsson's pioneering work in this country, *Finger Plays* (two words then) *for Nursery and Kindergarten*, copyright 1893, marked 90th Thousand, six years later, a most impressive figure now, let alone then. But more important is the fact that music abounds in this early work, arranged for the piano and voice, which also surprised me, because music in most fingerplay books I am familiar with is either subordinate or nonexistent. I don't know the reason for this; I suppose that as the years went by, playing the piano was not required of teachers of the very young, or that it became impractical to place a piano in the usual kindergarten-nursery room.

Which leads to this book. It was put together partially to redress this imbalance. While I was delighted to find out that music was so important to Froebel and to Poulsson from the earliest fingerplay days, playing the piano is not a prerequisite for enjoying the songs here. Guitar chords are provided for folk-guitarists (transpose to simpler keys where required, or use the capo). Or, just sing the songs *a cappella*. Or, pick them out one-finger style on any instrument. Also, it is not absolutely necessary for the children to sing the songs and do the fingerplays at the same time; do both where possible, or either, one at a time. The teacher or parent should use the book as a point of departure, not as a bible, and improvise and embellish and change to fit particular circumstances or needs.

As to the songs themselves: There are familiar fingerplay songs. There are also familiar fingerplays newly set to music, and there are some lovely unfamiliar songs and famous folksongs with brand-new fingerplays.

I would like to thank Robert Luce, who indirectly gave me the idea for the book; Susan Ginsberg, of the Bank Street College of Education; and Dean Amy Hostler and Professor Myrtle Searles of the Mills College of Education. I am grateful to them all for their sympathetic assistance.

Tom Glazer
Scarborough, N.Y. 1971-72

CONTENTS

Arranged alphabetically

To the children I've sung for and with,
and to those I haven't.

1 / THE BARNYARD SONG

Adapted by Tom Glazer

1. I had a bird and the bird pleased me, I fed my bird on yon-der tree. Bird goes fid-dle-ee - fee.

2. I had a hen and the hen pleased me, I fed my hen by yon-der tree.

3. I had a duck and the duck pleased me, I fed my duck by yon-der tree.

Hen goes chim-my chuck, chim-my chuck, Bird goes fid-dle-ee - fee.
Duck goes quack quack, quack quack,

Song 1.

4. I had a goose and the goose pleased me,
   I fed my goose by yonder tree.
   Goose goes swishy, swashy,
   Duck goes quack-quack, quack-quack,
   Hen goes chimmy chuck, chimmy chuck,
   Bird goes fid-dle-ee-fee.

5. I had a sheep and the sheep pleased me,
   I fed my sheep by yonder tree.
   Sheep goes baa-baa, baa-baa,
   Goose goes swishy, swashy,
   Duck goes quack-quack, quack-quack,
   Hen goes chimmy chuck, chimmy chuck,
   Bird goes fid-dle-ee-fee.

6. I had a pig and the pig pleased me,
   I fed my pig by yonder tree.
   Pig goes oink-oink, oink-oink,
   Sheep goes baa-baa, baa-baa,
   Goose goes swishy, swashy,
   Duck goes quack-quack, quack-quack,
   Hen goes chimmy chuck, chimmy chuck,
   Bird goes fid-dle-ee-fee.

7. I had a cow and the cow pleased me,
   I fed my cow by yonder tree.
   Cow goes moo-moo, moo-moo,
   Pig goes oink-oink, oink-oink,
   Sheep goes baa-baa, baa-baa,
   Goose goes swishy, swashy,
   Duck goes quack-quack, quack-quack,
   Hen goes chimmy chuck, chimmy chuck,
   Bird goes fid-dle-ee-fee.

8. I had a horse and the horse pleased me,
   I fed my horse by yonder tree.
   Horse goes neigh-neigh, neigh-neigh,
   Cow goes moo-moo, moo-moo,
   Pig goes oink-oink, oink-oink,
   Sheep goes baa-baa, baa-baa,
   Goose goes swishy, swashy,
   Duck goes quack-quack, quack-quack,
   Hen goes chimmy chuck, chimmy chuck,
   Bird goes fid-dle-ee-fee.

v. 1: Waving motion is made with one hand to imitate bird flying.
v. 2: First two fingers of one hand "walk" up other arm, to imitate hen walking.
v. 3: Fingers of one hand open and shut against thumb of same hand to imitate duck bill.
v. 4: Cross thumbs of both hands and wave hands to imitate goose flying.
v. 5: Forefingers of both hands go up and down with rest of hand closed to imitate sheep horns.
v. 6: Open and shut one hand rapidly in time with "oink, oink."
v. 7: Hold arm out loosely and wave forearm vertically to imitate cow's tail.
v. 8: Drum fingers on desk or table to imitate horse's hooves.

2/THE BEAR WENT OVER THE MOUNTAIN

Oh, the bear went o-ver the moun-tain, The bear went o-ver the

moun-tain, The bear went o-ver the moun-tain To see what he could see.

1. To see what he could see, _____ To see what he could see,
2. He saw the oth-er side, _____ He saw the oth-er side,

"Climb" with the fingers steeply up and then down, using one or both hands.

3 / BINGO

Have the children "write" each letter spelled out in the song, tracing the letter in the air, and slowing the song down for this purpose.

4 / BROTHER, COME AND DANCE WITH ME

From HANSEL AND GRETEL by Humperdinck   Adapted by Tom Glazer

Girls: Broth - er, come and dance with me, take our hands and one, two, three—

Right foot first, left foot, then round a - bout and back a - gain.

Boys: I will dance, but show me how, how to step and when to bow,

2. With your head you nod real quick,
   With your hands you click, click, click,
   First your head, then your hand,
   Click, click, click to beat the band.

3. With one eye you wink, wink, wink,
   With two eyes you blink, blink, blink,
   First you wink, then you blink,
   Frowning hard will help you think.

Show me, show me what to do, so that I can dance like you.

All: 1. With your foot you tap, tap, tap, with your hands you clap, clap, clap,

Right foot first, left foot, then round a-bout and back a-gain.

4. With you foot you tap, tap, tap,
   With your hands you clap, clap, clap,
   Right foot first, left foot, then
   Round about and back again.

If this song is not performed as a playparty song, with the children out of their seats, it can be done as a finger, hand and body play song while the children are seated, by simply suiting the action to the words. Instead of dancing, the children can hold hands and wave them together in time to the song, then do the rest as indicated: clapping, feet work, bowing, etc.

5 / THE BUS SONG

Adapted with new words by T.G.

1. The peo-ple in the bus go up and down, up and down, up and down. The peo-ple in the bus go up and down, All a-round the town. 2. The

wip-er on the bus goes, "Swish, swish, swish, swish, swish, swish, swish, swish, swish." The wip-er on the bus goes, "Swish, swish, swish," All a-round the town. 3. The

3. The brake on the bus goes, "Roomp, roomp, roomp,
Roomp, roomp, roomp, roomp, roomp, roomp!"
The brake on the bus goes, "Roomp, roomp, roomp!"
All around the town.

4. The money in the bus goes, "Clink, clink, clink,
Clink, clink, clink, clink, clink, clink!"
The money in the bus goes, "Clink, clink, clink!"
All around the town.

5. The wheels on the bus go 'round and around,
   'Round and around; 'round and around.
   The wheels on the bus go 'round and around,
   All around the town.

6. There's a baby in the bus goes, "Wah, wah, wah,
   Wah, wah, wah; wah, wah, wah!"
   There's a baby in the bus goes, "Wah, wah, wah!"
   All around the town.

7. There's a bus on the bus goes, "Bus, bus, bus,
   Bus, bus, bus; bus, bus, bus!"
   There's a bus on the bus goes, "Bus, bus, bus!"
   All around the town.

v. 1: Children go up and down in their seats.
v. 2: Hold arms out and imitate wipers by waving forearms.
v. 3: Pull an imaginary hand-brake up three times to "roomp, roomp, roomp."
v. 4: Tap thumb against forefinger (same hand) three times to "clink, clink, clink."
v. 5: Describe circles with both hands to "'round and around."
v. 6: "Rock" a baby in one's arms.
v. 7: Hold an imaginary wheel and "drive" the bus.

6 / CHARLIE OVER THE WATER

With energy   Words Anon. music T.G.

Char - lie o - ver the wa - ter, Char - lie o - ver the sea,

Char - lie catch a black - bird, can't catch me! _____

If there is a boy named Charlie in the class (or at home), point to him in rhythm, twice in each measure. On the word "catch" make a catching motion with one hand by quickly closing it. On the words "can't catch me," point at oneself on the word "me." If there is no Charlie, substitute another name, then repeat, using the names of all the children (and adults), one for each time.

7 / COME ON AND JOIN INTO THE GAME

Cheerfully

Adapted and arranged by Tom Glazer

1. Let ev - 'ry - one clap hands like me, *(Clap! Clap!)* Let ev - 'ry - one clap hands like me *(Clap! Clap!)*. Come on and join in - to the game, _____ you'll find that it's al - ways the same *(Clap! Clap!)*.

2. Let everyone laugh like me, *(Ha! Ha!)*
Let everyone laugh like me, *(Ha! Ha!)*
Come on and join into the game,
You'll find that it's always just the same
(Ha! Ha!)

3. Let everyone cry like me, *(Boo! Hoo!)*
Let everyone cry like me, *(Boo! Hoo!)*
Come on and join into the game,
You'll find that it's always just the same
(Boo! Hoo!)

4. Let everyone yawn like me, *(Yawn!)*
Let everyone yawn like me, *(Yawn!)*
Come on and join into the game,
You'll find that it's always just the same
(Yawn!)

5. Let everyone sleep like me, *(Yawn!)*
Let everyone sleep like me, *(Yawn!)*
Come on and join into the game,
You'll find that it's always just the same
(Yawn!)

Just do what the song indicates.

8 / THE DICKEY-BIRD SONG

New words and music by T.G.

1. Two lit - tle dick - ey - birds sat up - on a hill,
2. Two lit - tle dick - ey - birds sat so ver - y still,

One named Jack and the oth - er named Jill. Fly a - way, Jack,
One named Jack and the oth - er named Jill. Sing a song, Jack,

fly a - way, Jill, Come back, Jack, come back Jill.
sing a - long, Jill, I'll sing too, yes, I will.

Hold hands out, palms forward. Right hand waves and moves to the right on the words, "fly away, Jack"; then the left similarly on the words, "fly away, Jill." Each hand then "flies" back in turn with the next words. In verse two, hold both hands out again very quietly for a moment. On the words, "sing a song, Jack," open and shut right hand very quickly, followed by the left hand until the end of verse two.

9 / DOWN BY THE STATION

Let the children simply imitate pulling a throttle rhythmically. If they are up to it, they can also sing the song as a round in four parts, as indicated.

10 / EENTSY WEENTSY SPIDER

The een - tsy ween - tsy spi - der went up the wa - ter spout;

Down came the rain____ and washed the spi - der out;

Out came the sun____ and dried up all the rain; Now

een - tsy ween - tsy spi - der went up the spout a - gain.

SWIVEL THE FINGERS

Place each thumb against opposite forefinger of the other hand, then swivel the fingers alternately so that one pair of thumb-and-forefinger goes above, then the other pair, making a "climbing" motion. This on the first line. On line two drop the arms to the side while the fingers wiggle. On third line make a big circle with the hands clasped over the head for the sun. Repeat motion of line one for the last line.

11 / EYE WINKER

Moderately

Melody and new words by Tom Glazer

1. Eye wink - er, _____ Tom Tink - er, _____ nose
2. The head bone, _____ the neck bone, _____ the

smell - er, _____ mouth eat - er.
el - bow, _____ the knee bone. _____

Chin chop - per, chin chop - per, chin chop-per, chop-per chin.

3. The shoulder bone, the wrist bone,
   The chest bone, the rest bone
   Chin chopper, chin chopper,
   Chin chopper, chopper chin.

4. Eye winker, Tom Tinker,
   Nose smeller, mouth eater.
   Chin chopper, chin chopper,
   Chin chopper, chopper chin.

v. 1: Wink eye (or blink both) on line one. Sniff on line two. Chewing motions with mouth on line three. Nod head vigorously rest of verse.

v. 2 and 3: Point to each bone mentioned, and nod vigorously on chin-chopper words.

12 / FIVE LITTLE DUCKS

1. Five lit-tle ducks went swim-ming one day, o-ver the pond and far a-way.
2. Four lit-tle ducks went swim-ming one day, o-ver the pond and far a-way.

Moth-er duck said, "Quack, quack, quack, quack," But on - ly four lit - tle ducks came back.
Moth-er duck said, "Quack, quack, quack, quack," But on - ly three lit - tle ducks came back.

3. Three little ducks went swimming one day,
   Over the pond and far away.
   Mother duck said, "Quack, quack, quack, quack,"
   But only two little ducks came back.

4. Two little ducks went swimming one day,
   Over the pond and far away.
   Mother duck said, "Quack, quack, quack, quack,"
   But only one little duck came back.

5. One little duck went swimming one day,
   Over the pond and far away.
   Mother duck said, "Quack, quack, quack, quack,"
   But no little ducks came back.

6. Five little ducks came back one day,
   Over the pond and far away.
   Mother duck said, "Quack, quack, quack, quack,"
   As five little ducks came swimming back.

Make swimming motion with one hand away from body. On last line tuck thumb under hand and "swim" back toward body with only four fingers showing. This for verse one. In the other verses do similarly, dropping one finger more each time. (Use middle, ring and pinky for three fingers. Use first two fingers for two; forefinger for one. When "no" little ducks come back, do nothing.)

13 / GO IN AND OUT THE WINDOW

Actually a playparty song. If playpartying is not feasible, then simply point to self on the word "in" and away on the word "out." On the last line, open and shut a window in dumb-show, on the word "we" (open) and "-fore" (shut).

14 / GRANDMA'S SPECTACLES

Moderately

Words: Anon. Music: Tom Glazer

Here are grand-ma's spec - ta - cles, and here is grand-ma's hat, And
here's the way she folds her hands, and puts them in her lap.

Here are grand-pa's spec - ta - cles, and here is grand-pa's hat, And
here's the way he folds his arms and sits like that.

On the word "spectacles" make two circles with the hands and place them against the eyes.
Pat the head on the word "hat." Suit the remaining actions to the words.

15/HERE IS THE CHURCH

Moderately

Words: Anon. Music: Tom Glazer

Here is the church, here is the stee-ple, O-pen the doors and see all the peo-ple. Here is the par-son go-ing up-stairs, And here he is a - say-ing his prayers.

Each play of the fingers comes *after* each phrase of the song:
1. Interlace fingers with fingertips down and knuckles showing.
2. Unfold forefingers only to form an inverted "V" like a steeple.
3. Turn palms upward showing interlaced fingertips.
4. Wiggle interlaced fingers.
5. Unlace fingers. Form a "ladder" with one hand, fingers apart, and climb up ladder with first two fingers of other hand.
6. Form hands pointing upward together in a prayerlike position.

16 / HE'S GOT THE WHOLE WORLD IN HIS HANDS

Chorus:

He's got the whole world___ in His hands, He's got the whole wide world___ in His hands, He's got the whole world____ in His hands, He's got the whole world in His hands.____

1. He's got the little bitty baby in His hands,
   He's got the little bitty baby in His hands,
   He's got the little bitty baby in His hands,
   He's got the whole world in His hands.
   Chorus:

2. He's got you and me, brother, in His hands,
   He's got you and me, brother, in His hands,
   He's got you and me, brother, in His hands,
   He's got the whole world in His hands.
   Chorus:

1. Chorus: On words, "the whole world," describe a great globe with both hands. On words, "in his hands," lace fingers, palms up, and extend both arms in front. Repeat throughout chorus on the proper words.
2. v. 1: Rock a little baby in one's arms.
3. v. 2: Point to "you and me," and lace fingers again. Point to boys.
4. v. 3: Same as v. 2, pointing to girls.

17 / HICKORY DICKORY DOCK

Hick-o-ry, dick-o-ry, dock! The mouse ran up the

clock; The clock struck one, and down he run,

Hick-o-ry, dick-o-ry dock!

Raise both arms in front, elbows bent, hands near but not touching, **forearms parallel to floor.** On first line beat rhythm with both arms. On second line run first two **fingers of one hand up other arm. Point forefinger directly up on next line. Run fingers down forearm.** End by extending arms and beating the rhythm as in first line.

18 / HUSH LITTLE BABY

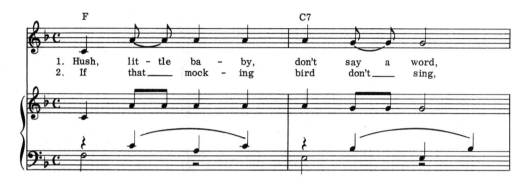

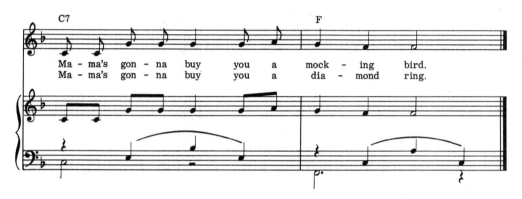

1. Hush, lit-tle ba-by, don't say a word,
   Ma-ma's gon-na buy you a mock-ing bird.

2. If that mock-ing bird don't sing,
   Ma-ma's gon-na buy you a dia-mond ring.

3. If that diamond ring turns brass,
   Mama's gonna buy you a looking-glass.

4. If that looking-glass gets broke,
   Mama's gonna buy you a billy goat.

5. If that billy goat don't pull,
   Mama's gonna buy you a cart 'n' bull.

6. If that cart 'n' bull turn over,
   Mama's gonna buy you a dog named Rover.

7. If that dog named Rover don't bark,
   Mama's gonna buy you a horse 'n' cart.

8. If that horse 'n' cart fall down,
   You'll be the sweetest little baby in town.

v. 1: Rock a cradle with one hand, while making a shushing gesture with forefinger of other hand against lips.

v. 2: Wave one hand quickly several times while moving it away, like a bird flying.

v. 3: Make circle with thumb and forefinger of one hand and place on finger of other hand, as a ring.

v. 4: Place hands up in front, palms facing yourself. Throw hands down on words "gets broke."

v. 5: Tug very hard on lines.

v. 6: Make circular motions with hands going around each other.

v. 7: With one hand keep thumb pointing up, palm perpendicular to floor, fingers open in the middle only. (Hand looks like dog in this position.)

v. 8: Throw hands and arms downward, then make a kissing sound.

19 / I KNOW AN OLD LADY

1. I know an old la-dy who swal-lowed a fly, I don't know why she swal-lowed a fly, Per-haps she'll die. 2. I know an old la-dy who swal-lowed a spi-der that wrig-gled and wrig-gled and tick-led in-side her; She swal-lowed the spi-der to catch the fly, But I don't know why she

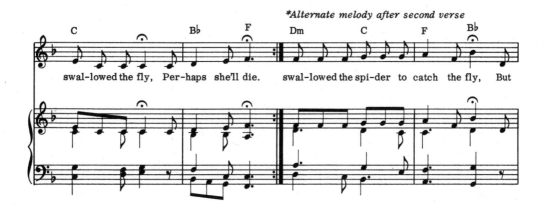

Alternate melody after second verse

swal-lowed the fly, Per-haps she'll die.   swal-lowed the spi-der to catch the fly, But

3. I know an old lady who swallowed a bird,
Now, ain't it absurd to swallow a bird?
She swallowed the bird to catch the spider,
She swallowed the spider to catch the fly,
But I don't know why she swallowed the fly,
Perhaps she'll die.

4. I know an old lady who swallowed a cat,
Now fancy that, to swallow a cat!
She swallowed the cat to catch the bird,
She swallowed the bird to catch the spider,
She swallowed the spider to catch the fly,
But I don't know why she swallowed the fly,
Perhaps she'll die.

5. I know an old lady who swallowed a dog,
Oh, what a hog to swallow a dog!
She swallowed the dog to catch the cat,
She swallowed the cat to catch the bird,
She swallowed the bird to catch the spider,
She swallowed the spider to catch the fly,
But I don't know why she swallowed the fly,
Perhaps she'll die.

6. I know an old lady who swallowed a cow,
I don't know how she swallowed a cow.
She swallowed the cow to catch the dog,
She swallowed the dog to catch the cat,
She swallowed the cat to catch the bird,
She swallowed the bird to catch the spider,
She swallowed the spider to catch the fly,
But I don't know why she swallowed the fly,
Perhaps she'll die.

7. I know an old lady who swallowed a horse,
(Spoken) SHE DIED, OF COURSE!

On the words "I know an old lady," place folded hands under chin. Swallow on the word
"swallow" where it appears. Make a catching motion when the word "catch" appears. Shrug
on the words "I don't know why." And look sad on the words "perhaps she'll die."

20 / I'M A LITTLE TEA-POT

1. I'm a lit-tle tea-pot short and stout, here is my han-dle, here is my spout.
2. I'm a ver-y spe-cial pot it's true, here, let me show you what it can do.

When I get all steamed up then I shout, tip me o-ver and pour me out.
I can change my han-dle and my spout, tip me o-ver and pour me out.

Act very stout. Place one hand on hip. Extend other arm, elbow and wrist bent. Nod head vigorously. Tip sideward in direction of extended arm. In second verse, reverse hand on hip and extended arm, and tip in the other direction.

21 / I ROLL THE BALL

By R. Abrashkin

Lyrics under the music:

I roll the ball to Dad-dy, he rolls the ball to me. I
roll the ball to Mom-my, she rolls the ball to me.
Roll the ball, roll the ball, roll the ball, roll the ball. I

2. I roll the ball to teacher, she rolls the ball to me...

3. I roll the ball to my friend, he (she) rolls the ball to me...

Can be acted out with a real ball and children and/or adults playing themselves or parts indicated in song. Or it can be done from the seats with an imaginary ball, in pairs.

22 / JACK AND JILL

1. Jack and Jill went up the hill, To fetch a pail of wa - ter;
Jack fell down and broke his crown, And Jill came tumb - ling af - ter.

2. Then up Jack got, and home did trot
As fast as he could caper,
To old Dame Dob, who patched his nob
With vinegar and brown paper.

3. Then Jill came in, and she did grin
To see Jack's paper plaster;
Her mother whipped her across her knee
For laughing at Jack's disaster.

Extend both arms and climb up using first two fingers of both hands. Quickly put one hand down on the words, "Jack fell down," then the other hand down more slowly, wiggling the fingers. In verse two, raise one arm quickly, then "run" with first two fingers. Slap one palm against head. In verse three, "walk" Jill in with two fingers, grin, then pretend to spank across the knees.

CLIMB UP

RUN

23 / JACK-O-LANTERN

Medium tempo

Words: Anon. Music: Tom Glazer

1. I'm a Jack-o'-lan-tern with a great big grin,
2. Five lit-tle Jack-o'-lan-terns sit-ting on a gate, The

I'm a Jack-o'-lan-tern with a can-dle in.
first one said, "Oh, my it's get-ting late."

is our chance." 5. When "Whooo," went the wind and out went the

light, And a-way rode the witch on Hal-low-een night!

3. The second one said, "Let's have some fun."
   The third one said, "Let's run, run, run."

4. The fourth one said, "Let's dance, let's prance."
   The fifth one said, "Now is our chance."

v. 1: Grin exaggeratedly, then stick a forefinger on the top of the head, still grinning.

v. 2: Raise left arm, left palm facing yourself, fingers together. Place heel of other hand atop first hand, palm outward, fingers spread out, fanwise. Then shake one forefinger admonishingly in rhythm, on second line of the verse.

v. 3: Raise two fingers and wave arm back and forth rhythmically; then three fingers similarly.

v. 4: Raise four fingers and waggle them. Raise five fingers, make a fist and thrust upward strongly.

v. 5: Make blowing motion with mouth; shut both eyes, then raise both arms outward, wiggling all fingers.

24 / JENNIE JENKINS

1. Will you wear white, oh my dear, oh my dear? Will you wear white, Jen-nie Jen - kins? No, I won't wear white, for the col-lor's too bright, I'll buy me a fol-de-rol-de til-de-tol-de seek a dou-ble use a cause a roll a find me, Roll, Jen-nie Jen-kins,

2. Will you wear green, oh my dear, oh my dear,
Will you wear green, Jennie Jenkins?
No, I won't wear green; it ain't fit to be seen,
I'll buy me a folderolde tildetolde
Seek-a-double-use-a-cause-a-roll-a-find-me,
Roll, Jennie Jenkins, roll.

3. Will you wear blue, oh my dear, oh my dear,
Will you wear blue, Jennie Jenkins?
No, I won't wear blue, 'cause blue won't do,
I'll buy me a folderolde tildetolde
Seek-a-double-use-a-cause-a-roll-a-find-me,
Roll, Jennie Jenkins, roll.

4. Will you wear red, oh my dear, oh my dear,
Will you wear red, Jennie Jenkins?
No, I won't wear red; it's the color of my head,
I'll buy me a folderolde tildetolde
Seek-a-double-use-a-cause-a-roll-a-find-me,
Roll, Jennie Jenkins, roll.

5. Will you wear purple, oh my dear, oh my dear,
Will you wear purple, Jennie Jenkins?
No, I won't wear purple; it's the color of a turtle,
I'll buy me a folderolde tildetolde
Seek-a-double-use-a-cause-a-roll-a-find-me,
Roll, Jennie Jenkins, roll.

In every verse: point to the color named on anyone wearing that color, or on any object in the room. On the word "no," shake the head negatively. On the last line (the same in every verse) make a rolling motion with one hand.

25 / LITTLE ARABELLA MILLER

Rather slow

Words: Anon. Music: Adapted

Lit - tle Ar - a - bel - la Mill - er found a wool - ly cat - ter - pil - lar.

First it crawled up - on her moth - er, then up - on her ba - by broth - er;

All said, "Ar - a - bel - la Mill - er, take a - way that cat - er - pil - lar."

Extend one arm downward all the way, palm down, in the gesture indicating smallness. Wriggle one finger, like a caterpillar. Crawl with two fingers up one forearm, then reverse hand and arm. On the words "take away...," make a quick dismissing motion with one hand.

26 / THE LITTLE WHITE DUCK

Words: Walt Barrows Music: Bernard Zaretsky

1. There's a lit-tle white duck sit-ting in the wa - ter, A
lit-tle green frog swim-ming in the wa - ter, A

lit - tle white duck do-ing what he ought - er; He
lit - tle green frog do-ing what he ought - er; He

took a bite of a li - ly pad, Flapped his wings and he
jumped right off of the li - ly pad, that The lit-tle duck bit and he

said, "I'm glad I'm a lit-tle white duck sit-ting in the wa - ter,"
said, "I'm glad I'm a lit-tle green frog swim-ming in the wa - ter,"

quack,   quack,   quack.   2. There's a   boo.
glumph,   glumph,   glumph.

3. There's a little black bug floating on the water,
A little black bug doing what he ought-er,
He tickled the frog on the lily pad
That the little duck bit and he said, "I'm glad
I'm a little black bug floating on the water. Chirp, chirp, chirp."

4. There's a little red snake lying in the water,
A little red snake doing what he ought-er,
He frightened the duck and the frog so bad
He ate the little bug and he said, "I'm glad
I'm a little red snake lying in the water. Sss, sss, sss."

5. Now there's nobody left sitting in the water,
Nobody left doing what he ought-er,
There's nothing left but the lily pad,
The duck and the frog ran away. It's sad
That there's nobody left sitting in the water. Boo, boo, boo.

v. 1: Fold hands and place in front. On "he took a bite," remove one hand and quickly close fingers against thumb. Cross thumbs and wiggle hands (flapping wings).

v. 2: Make swim-motion with one hand up and down. Throw same hand out suddenly, then back to swimming motion.

v. 3: Wave pinky, then tickle motion with forefinger, then wave pinky again.

v. 4: Extend and undulate one arm. Make "eating" motion with fingers and thumb of same hand, then back to first motion.

v. 5: Shrug, while both arms are out, palms up, and look sad.

27 / THE MORE WE ARE TOGETHER

Arranged with new words by Tom Glazer

The more we are to-geth-er, to-geth-er, to-geth-er, The more we are to-geth-er the hap-pi-er we'll be. For your friends are my friends, and my friends are your friends. The more we are to-geth-er, the hap-pi-er we'll be.

2. The more we work together, together, together,
   The more we work together, the happier we'll be.
   For working together, is having fun together,
   The more we work together, the happier we'll be.

3. The more we share together, together, together,
   The more we share together, the happier we'll be.
   For sharing is caring, and caring is sharing,
   The more we share together, the happier we'll be.

v. 1: Hug yourself and sway rhythmically, side to side. Point with both forefingers to "your friends," then touch yourself on "my friends," then back to hugging. 2: Clasp hands and move them in time to music. Shake hands with person nearest you, or **everyone** hold hands.

28 / THE MULBERRY BUSH

1. Here we go 'round the mul - ber - ry bush, The mul - ber - ry bush, The
3. This is the way we i - ron our clothes, i - ron our clothes,

mul - ber - ry bush, Here we go 'round the mul - ber - ry bush so
i - ron our clothes, This is the way we i - ron our clothes so

ear - ly in ___ the morn - ing. 2. This is the way we
ear - ly in ___ the morn - ing. 4. This is the way we

scrub our clothes, we scrub our clothes, we scrub our clothes,
hang our clothes, we hang our clothes, we hang our clothes,

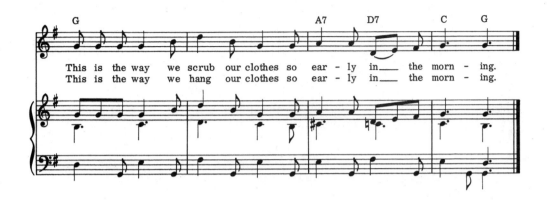

This is the way   we scrub   our clothes so   ear - ly in___ the morn - ing.
This is the way   we hang   our clothes so   ear - ly in___ the morn - ing.

Describe circle with a finger. In succeeding verses, simply act out with the hands the various activities indicated.

29 / THE MUSICIANS

March tempo

By Chas. Grean and Tom Glazer

1. I am a fine mu - si - cian, I prac-tice ev-'ry day, And
2. I am a fine mu - si - cian, and I get lots of pay, 'Cause

peo - ple come from miles a - round just to hear me play my
peo - ple throw me pen - nies, when they hear me play my

trum - pet, my trum - pet, they love to hear my trum - pet. Ta -
tu - ba, my tu - ba, they love to hear my tu - ba.

1. *like a trumpet*

ra - ta-ta, ta - ra - ta-ta, ta - ra - ta - ta - ta - ta.

2. *like a tuba*   *to 1st ending*

oom - pah, oom - pah, oom - pah, oom - pah, oom - pah - pah. Ta

3. *like a trombone*   *to 2nd & 1st endings*

Dah, dah, dah dah dah, dah dah dah dah dah dah.

more

Every verse: clap in rhythm until chorus, in which imitate playing the instrument, viz., hold trumpet with left hand and wiggle fingers near mouth to press valves or keys; for the tuba, right hand moves away from mouth to side and presses keys; left hand holds instrument. For trombone, right hand makes sliding motions out and back; left hand holds. For piccolo, both hands go up to right side of mouth; fingers wiggle, with left palm facing in, right one facing out. On last verse, everyone becomes a conductor and leads the band.

3. I am a fine musician; my music is so gay,
And everybody dances when they hear me play
My trombone, my trombone,
The love to hear my trombone.
Dah dah, dah dah dah, dah dah dah dah, dah-dah.
Oom-pah, oom-pah, oom-pah, oom-pah, oom-pah-pah.
Ta-ra-ta-ta, ta-ra-ta-ta, ta-ra-ta-ta-ta-ta.

4. I am a fine musician, that's what the people say,
And all the children follow mè when they hear me play
My piccolo, my piccolo,
They love to hear my piccolo.
Dee, dee, dee, dee-dle, dee, dee, dee, dee-dle, dee-dle, dee, dee, dee-dle, dee-dle, dee.
Dah dah, dah dah dah, dah dah dah dah, dah-dah.
Oom-pah, oom-pah, oom-pah, oom-pah, oom-pah-pah.
Ta-ra-ta-ta, ta-ra-ta-ta, ta-ra-ta-ta-ta-ta.

*5. I am a fine musician, I practice every day,
    And if you'd like to play with me, I'll show you the way,
    Come join me, come join me,
    Just take a part and join me.
    Ta-ra-ta-ta, ta-ra-ta-ta, ta-ra-ta-ta-ta-ta.
    Oom-pah, oom-pah, oom-pah, oom-pah, oom-pah-pah.
    Dah dah, dah dah dah, dah dah dah dah, dah-dah.
    Dee, dee, dee, dee-dle, dee, dee, dee, dee-dle, dee-dle, dee, dee, dee-dle, dee-dle, dee.

*All the parts which imitate instruments can be sung simultaneously as a 2, 3, or 4-part chorus,
 or consecutively in unison, if the children are too young.

30 / OLD MACDONALD

1. Old Mac-Don-ald had a farm, E - I - E - I - O; And
2. Old Mac-Don-ald had a farm, E - I - E - I - O; And

on his farm he had a cow, E - I - E - I - O; With a
on his farm he had a pig, E - I - E - I - O; With an

Repeat as necessary

moo-moo here and a moo-moo there, here a moo, there a moo, ev-'rywhere a moo-moo,
oink-oink here and an oink-oink there, here an oink, there an oink, ev-'rywhere an oink-oink,

Old Mac-Don-ald had a farm, E - I - E - I - O.

3. Old MacDonald had a farm, E-I-E-I-O;
   And on his farm he had a duck, E-I-E-I-O;
   With a quack-quack here and a quack-quack there,
   Here a quack, there a quack, ev'rywhere a quack-quack,
   An oink-oink here and an oink-oink there,
   Here an oink, there an oink, ev'rywhere an oink-oink,
   A moo-moo here and a moo-moo there,
   Here a moo, there a moo, ev'rywhere a moo-moo,
   Old MacDonald had a farm, E-I-E-I-O.

4. Old MacDonald had a farm, E-I-E-I-O;
   And on his farm he had a horse, E-I-E-I-O;
   With a neigh-neigh here and a neigh-neigh there,
   Here a neigh, there a neigh, ev'rywhere a neigh-neigh,
   A quack-quack here and a quack-quack there,
   Here a quack, there a quack, ev'rywhere a quack-quack,
   An oink-oink here and an oink-oink there,
   Here an oink, there an oink, ev'rywhere an oink-oink,
   A moo-moo here and a moo-moo there,
   Here a moo, there a moo, ev'rywhere a moo-moo,
   Old MacDonald had a farm, E-I-E-I-O.

5. Old MacDonald had a farm, E-I-E-I-O;
   And on his farm he had a donkey, E-I-E-I-O;
   With a hee-haw here and a hee-haw there,
   Here a hee-haw, there a hee-haw, ev'rywhere a hee-haw,
   A neigh-neigh here and a neigh-neigh there,
   Here a neigh, there a neigh, ev'rywhere a neigh-neigh,
   A quack-quack here and a quack-quack there
   Here a quack, there a quack, ev'rywhere a quack-quack,
   An oink-oink here and an oink-oink there,
   Here an oink, there an oink, ev'rywhere an oink-oink,
   A moo-moo here and a moo-moo there,
   Here a moo, there a moo, ev'rywhere a moo-moo,
   Old MacDonald had a farm, E-I-E-I-O.

6. Old MacDonald had a farm, E-I-E-I-O;
   And on his farm he had some chickens, E-I-E-I-O;
   With a chick-chick here and a chick-chick there,
   Here a chick, there a chick, ev'rywhere a chick-chick,
   A hee-haw here and a hee-haw there
   Here a hee-haw, there a hee-haw, ev'rywhere a hee-haw,
   A neigh-neigh here and a neigh-neigh there,
   Here a neigh, there a neigh, ev'rywhere a neigh-neigh,
   A quack-quack here and a quack-quack there
   Here a quack, there a quack, ev'rywhere a quack-quack,
   An oink-oink here and an oink-oink there,
   Here an oink, there an oink, ev'rywhere an oink-oink,
   A moo-moo here and a moo-moo there,
   Here a moo, there a moo, ev'rywhere a moo-moo,
   Old MacDonald had a farm, E-I-E-I-O.

(Add your own animals)

Sing and/or clap in each verse until the chorus. In each chorus symbolize each animal, e.g.,
pull udders for the cow; press one finger under the nose upward and pull down under-part
of eyes with thumb and finger of other hand at the same time, to imitate a pig;
wiggle-waggle the upper part of the body for a duck; a riding motion for a horse; a hand on
either side of the head for a donkey's ears, etc.

31 / ON TOP OF SPAGHETTI

By Tom Glazer

On top of spa - ghet - ti, ____
ta - ble ____

____ all cov - ered with cheese, ____
and on - to the floor, ____

____ I lost my poor meat - ball, ____
____ And then my poor meat - ball ____

____ when some - bod - y sneezed.
____ rolled out of the door. ____

(last time only)

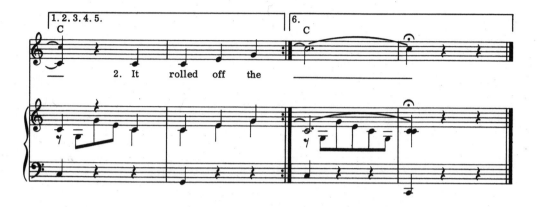

2. It rolled off the

3. It rolled in the garden and under a bush,
   And then my poor meatball was nothing but mush.

4. The mush was as tasty as tasty could be,
   And early next summer it grew into a tree.

5. The tree was all covered with beautiful moss,
   It grew lovely meatballs and tomato sauce.

6. So if you eat spaghetti, all covered with cheese,
   Hold on to your meatballs and don't ever sneeze.

Make up appropriate finger and body actions for the words, and don't leave out a real, live sneeze.

32 / PAT-A-CAKE

Words: Anon. Music: Tom Glazer

Can be done alone or in pairs with one child (or adult) moving the hands of the other, viz.: pat the hands twice in the first measure, on the first and third beat; three times in the second measure, on the first, second, and third beat, following the tune. The same with measures three and four. Make a rolling motion on "roll it," then a pat and write "B", then throw arms out on last line.

33 / PETER HAMMERS

With good accent

Pe - ter ham-mers with one ham - mer, one ham - mer, one ham - mer;

Pe - ter ham-mers with one ham - mer all day long.

2. Peter hammers with two hammers, two hammers, two hammers;
   Peter hammers with two hammers all day long.

3. Peter hammers with three hammers, three hammers, three hammers;
   Peter hammers with three hammers all day long.

4. Peter hammers with four hammers, four hammers, four hammers;
   Peter hammers with four hammers all day long.

5. Peter hammers with five hammers, five hammers, five hammers;
   Peter hammers with five hammers all day long.

(very slow)
6. Peter's very tired now, tired now, tired now;
   Peter's very tired now, all day long.

(fast)
7. Peter's wide awake now, awake now, awake now;
   Peter's wide awake now, all day long.

v. 1: Hammer with one fist in rhythm. 2: With two fists. 3: With two fists and one foot.
4: With two fists and both feet. 5: With two feet, holding up one hand palm out.
6: No hammering at all. 7: With both feet and hands faster.

34 / PICK A BALE OF COTTON

2. Me and my brother, we can pick a bale of cotton,
   Me and my brother, we can pick a bale a day.
   Chorus:

3. Me and my sister, we can pick a bale of cotton,
   Me and my sister, we can pick a bale a day.
   Chorus:

4. I can pick a, pick a, pick a, pick a bale of cotton,
   I can pick a, pick a, pick a, pick a bale a day.
   Chorus:

v. 1: Jump down, turn around and clap in rhythm. 2: Clap both hands against hands of a
partner in rhythm. 3: Do the same with another partner, or with the same one.
4: Reach out with hands alternately, making a picking motion with fingers.

35 / POP GOES THE WEASEL

All a-round the cob-bler's bench, The mon-key chased the wea-sel. The mon-key thought 'twas all__ in fun. Pop! goes the wea-sel. A pen-ny for a spool__ of thread, A pen-ny for a nee-dle, That's the way the mon-ey goes, Pop! Goes the wea-sel.

Make circle with finger round and round, on line one. Chase the weasel by letting one hand run after the other with first two fingers of either hand "running." On the word "pop," clap the hands sharply once. Make sewing motions, ending with another clap on the word "pop."

36 / PUT YOUR FINGER IN THE AIR

By Woody Guthrie

1. Put your fin-ger in the air, in the air, Put your
2. Put your fin-ger on your head, on your head, Put your

fin-ger in the air, in the air; Put your
fin-ger on your head, on your head; Put your

fin-ger in the air, and leave it a-bout a year, Put your
fin-ger on your head, tell me is it green or red, Put your

fin-ger in the air, in the air.
fin-ger on your head, on your head.

3. Put your finger on your nose, on your nose,
Put your finger on your nose, on your nose;
Put your finger on your nose
And let the cold wind blow,
Put your finger on your nose, on your nose.

4. Put your finger on your shoe, on your shoe,
Put your finger on your shoe, on your shoe,
Put your finger on your shoe
And leave it a day or two,
Put your finger on your shoe, on your shoe.

5. Put your finger on your chin, on your chin,
Put your finger on your chin, on your chin;
Put your finger on your chin,
That's where the food slips in,
Put your finger on your chin, on your chin.

6. Put your finger on your cheek, on your cheek,
Put your finger on your cheek, on your cheek;
Put your finger on your cheek
And leave it about a week,
Put your finger on your cheek, on your cheek.

7. Put your fingers all together, all together,
Put your fingers all together, all together;
Put your fingers all together
And we'll clap for better weather,
Put your fingers all together, all together.

Just do what the words say.

37 / SAILING AT HIGH TIDE

With a swing

Adapted and arranged by Tom Glazer

1. Sail-ing in the boat when the tide runs high, Sail-ing in the
2. Here_ she_ comes so _ fresh and fair, Sky_ blue_
   (he)

boat when the tide runs high, Sail-ing in the boat when the
eyes and _ cur - ly hair, Ros - y in the cheek, and a

Repeat 1st Verse

tide_ runs_ high, Wait-ing for my good _ friend to come by'm bye.
dim-ple in her chin, Don't you be so mean,_ or you can't come in.
   (his)

Hold last note

1: Sway in time from side to side. 2: Point to favorite person, first beat, first and second measure, twice in third measure, once in fourth measure. Same routine next four measures. Point to cheek, then chin. Point finger admonishingly to the end in tempo. 3: Repeat first verse.

38 / SHOEMAKER, SHOEMAKER

Additional lyrics and melody by Tom Glazer

Energetically; but not fast

1. Shoe - mak - er, shoe - mak - er, mend my shoe, get it done by half - past two. My big toe is peep - ing through, Shoe - mak - er, shoe - mak - er, mend my shoe.

2. Shoe - mak - er, shoe - mak - er, what a hole, do not lose your self - con - trol, Bless my heel and bless my soul, Shoe - mak - er, shoe - mak - er, make it whole.

Repeat 1st Verse

Bang on desk or something similar with one fist in time with the accents of the words throughout.

39 / THE TAILOR AND THE MOUSE

Medium tempo

1. There was a tail-or had a mouse, Hi did-dle um-kum feed-le. They
2. The tail-or thought the mouse was ill, Hi did-dle um-kum feed-le. He

lived to-geth-er in one house, Hi did-dle um-kum feed-le.
give him part of a blue pill, Hi did-dle um-kum feed-le.

Chorus:

Hi did-dle um-kum tar-um tan-tum, in the town of Ram-sey,

Hi did-dle um-kum o-ver the lea, Hi did-dle um-kum feed-le.

3. The tailor thought his mouse would die,
   Hi diddle umkum feedle.
   He baked him in an apple pie,
   Hi diddle umkum feedle.
   Chorus:

4. The pie was cut, the mouse ran out,
   Hi diddle umkum feedle.
   The tailor followed him all about,
   Hi diddle umkum feedle.
   Chorus:

1: Sewing motion with one hand. Make a mouse with the other hand by making a fist, but with thumb *under* forefinger. Clap in tempo throughout every chorus. 2: Look at wristwatch or bare wrist, like a doctor; pop pill in mouth. 3: Hold head in both hands and shake head from side to side. 4: Cut pie with one hand; make running motion with the other.

40 / TEN FINGERS

Words: Anon. Music: Tom Glazer

Show all fingers by holding hands up, then suit the rest of the action to the words.

41 / TEN LITTLE INDIANS

One lit-tle, two lit-tle, three lit-tle In-dians;
Ten lit-tle, nine lit-tle, eight lit-tle In-dians;

four lit-tle, five lit-tle, six lit-tle In-dians; Seven lit-tle, eight lit-tle
seven lit-tle, six lit-tle, five lit-tle In-dians, Four lit-tle, three lit-tle

nine lit-tle In-dians, Ten lit-tle In-dian boys.
two lit-tle In-dains, One lit-tle In-dian boy.

Put one finger up on the word "one," two fingers on "two," and so on through ten, using both hands, of course. Then reverse, following the words.

43 / THERE WAS A LITTLE TURTLE

Not fast

Words: Vachel Lindsay, Music: Tom Glazer

There was a lit-tle tur-tle; he lived in a box. He
swam in a pud-dle, he climbed on the rocks. He
snapped at a mos-qui-to; he snapped at a flea. He
caught the mos-qui-to; he caught the flea. He
snapped at a min-now and he snapped at me. (He)
caught the min-now and he did-n't catch me.

CLIMB WITH FINGERS OVER FINGERS

SNAP

(Each action is done on each successive line) Make fist, but with thumb under forefinger. Make a box motion with both hands. Make same fist and make swimming motion with it. Climb with fingers over other fingers. Snap with fingers and thumb of one hand three times facing out, and the fourth time at yourself, always on the word "snapped." Make three "catching" motions by closing fist quickly. On last line make several rapid catching motions at yourself, but keep dodging your head aside.

42 / THERE'S A HOLE IN THE BOTTOM OF THE SEA

*Each succeeding verse adds one more object in the first measure

2. There's a log in the hole, in the bottom of the sea...

3. There's a bump on the log, in the hole, in the bottom of the sea...

4. There's a frog on the bump, on the log, in the hole, in the bottom of the sea...

5. There's a wart on the frog, on the bump, on the log, in the hole, in the bottom of the sea...

6. There's a hair on the wart, on the frog, on the bump, on the log, in the hole, in the bottom of the sea...

7. There's a flea on the hair, on the wart, on the frog, on the bump, on the log, in the hole, in the bottom of the sea...

8. There's a germ on the flea, on the hair, on the wart, on the frog, on the bump, on the log, in the hole, in the bottom of the sea...

9. There's a *(grunt!)* on the germ, on the flea, on the hair, on the wart, on the frog, on the bump, on the log, in the hole, in the bottom of the sea...

v. 1: Describe circle with forefinger pointing downward. 2: Hold forearm up. 3: Slam fist down on the word "bump." 4: Hold fist up then slam down on word "bump." 5: Make small circle in front of you with thumb and finger. 6: Point to hair. 7: Hold pinky up. 8: Hold forefinger just over thumb without touching. 9: Grunt or squeak. (Don't forget to repeat circle-with-forefinger motion at end of each verse, pointing downward.)

44 / THIS LITTLE PIG

Words: Anon. Music: Tom Glazer

Medium tempo

This lit-tle pig went to mark-et, this lit-tle pig stayed home.

This lit-tle pig had roast beef, this lit-tle pig had none. But

this lit-tle pig cried, "Wee, wee, wee," all ____ the way home, But

all ____ the way home.

Point to thumb, then the other fingers in turn. When you get to the pinky, on the words "wee, wee, wee," tickle yourself.

45 / THIS OLD MAN

1. This old man, he played one, He played knick - knack
2. This old man, he played two, He played knick - knack

on my thumb, With a knick - knack, pad - dy wack,
on my shoe, With a knick - knack, pad - dy wack,

give the dog a bone, This old man came roll - ing home.
give the dog a bone, This old man came roll - ing home.

3. This old man, he played three,
   He played knick-knack on my knee,
   With a knick-knack, paddy wack,
   Give the dog a bone,
   This old man came rolling home.

4. This old man, he played four,
   He played knick-knack on my door,
   With a knick-knack, paddy wack,
   Give the dog a bone,
   This old man came rolling home.

5. This old man, he played five,
   He played knick-knack on my hive,
   With a knick-knack, paddy wack,
   Give the dog a bone,
   This old man came rolling home.

6. This old man, he played six,
   He played knick-knack on my sticks,
   With a knick-knack, paddy wack,
   Give the dog a bone,
   This old man came rolling home.

7. This old man, he played seven,
   He played knick-knack up in heaven,
   With a knick-knack, paddy wack,
   Give the dog a bone,
   This old man came rolling home.

8. This old man, he played eight,
   He played knick-knack on my gate,
   With a knick-knack, paddy wack,
   Give the dog a bone,
   This old man came rolling home.

9. This old man, he played nine,
   He played knick-knack on my vine,
   With a knick-knack, paddy wack,
   Give the dog a bone,
   This old man came rolling home.

10. This old man, he played ten,
    He played knick-knack all over again,
    With a knick-knack, paddy wack,
    Give the dog a bone,
    This old man came rolling home.

1: Hold up one finger. Touch thumbs rhythmically. Tap knees on "knick-knack," (two taps); clap hands (twice) on "paddy-whack," and put one hand out on "give the dog a bone." Roll hands around each other on "this old man came rolling home." 2: Hold up two fingers. Tap shoes; the rest as above. 3: Hold up three fingers. Tap knee; the rest as above. 4: As above; open an imaginary door. 5: As above; make a hive shape with hands. 6: Wiggle fingers for sticks. 7: Point up to Heaven. 8: Open and shut imaginary gate. 9: Crawl fingers along imaginary vine, or use a variant: spine, and point to it. 10: Throw arms out.

46 / THIS TRAIN

With good rhythm

Adaptation with new words by Tom Glazer

This train is bound for glo - ry, this train,

This train is bound for glo - ry, this train,___

This train is bound for glo - ry, don't ride no one but the good and ho - ly,

This train is bound for glo - ry, this train.

simile throughout

rit.

2. This bike is rolling down hill, this bike,
   This bike is rolling down hill, this bike,
   This bike is rolling down hill,
   Over the bridge and by the old mill,
   This bike is rolling down hill, this bike.

3. This car belongs to daddy, this car,
   This car belongs to daddy, this car,
   This car belongs to daddy,
   When it's dirty, daddy gets maddy,
   This car belongs to daddy, this car.

4. This plane is flying so fast, this plane,
   This plane is flying so fast, this plane,
   This plane is flying so fast,
   Look real hard or it'll fly, fly right past,
   This plane is flying so fast, this plane.

5. This boat can sail to China, this boat,
   This boat can sail to China, this boat,
   This boat can sail to China,
   Woo, woo, woo, says the ocean liner,
   This boat can sail to China, this boat.

Imitate driving each vehicle, while moving body rhythmically. On the words, "this train," "this bike," etc., point twice at one's vehicle, once on each word.

47 WHAT WILL WE DO WITH THE BABY-O?

Rhythmically

Adapted by Tom Glazer

1. What will we do with the ba - by - o? What will we do with the ba - by - o?
2. Wind blows high and the wind blows low, Where, oh where does the old wind go?

What will we do with the ba - by - o? Send him to his dad - dy - o.
What will we do with the ba - by - o? Send him to his dad - dy - o.

3. Down in the hollow the cowbells ring,
   Bullfrogs jump and the jay-birds sing.
   What will we do with the baby-o?
   Send him to his daddy-o.

4. Bullfrog croaked and jumped up high,
   Jumped and jumped 'til he caught a fly.
   What will we do with the baby-o?
   Send him to his daddy-o.

1: Rock baby in arms in tempo. 2: Throw arms out and up on "high," and in and down on "low,"; the same through rest of verse. 3: Point to a hollow and ring a bell. Close fist and throw up high; move fingers back and forth against thumb to imitate birds singing. 4: Using fist for bullfrog, act out the words as indicated.

48 / WHEN I WAS A SHOEMAKER

With a swing; not fast

New words by Tom Glazer

1. When I was a shoe-mak-er, and a shoe-mak-er was I,
2. When I was a gen-tle-man, and a gen-tle-man was I,

I went this-a-way, and-a-this-a-way, and-a-this-a-way, went I.

3. When I was a lady,
   And a lady was I,
   I went this-a-way, and-a-this-a-way,
   And-a-this-a-way, went I.

4. When I was a teacher,
   And a teacher was I,
   I went this-a-way, and-a-this-a-way,
   And-a-this-a-way, went I.

5. When I was a doctor,
   And a doctor was I,
   I went this-a-way, and-a-this-a-way,
   And-a-this-a-way, went I.

1: Tap with fist in tempo. 2: Bow in tempo. 3: Curtsey, or wave arms grandly about.
4: Shake a forefinger in tempo at others. 5: Raise someone's wrist and look at your own
wrist.

49 / WHERE IS THUMBKIN?

1. Where is thumb - kin? Where is thumb - kin?
2. Where is point - er? Where is point - er?

Here I am, here I am; How are you to-day, sir?
Here I am, here I am; How are you to-day, sir?

Ver - y well I thank you, Run a - way, run a - way.
Ver - y well I thank you, Run a - way, run a - way.

3. Where is middle? Where is middle?
   Here I am, here I am;
   How are you today, sir?
   Very well, I thank you,
   Run away, run away.

4. Where is ringer? Where is ringer?
   Here I am, here I am;
   How are you today, sir?
   Very well, I thank you,
   Run away, run away.

5. Where is Pinky?...etc.

Place hands behind back. Show one thumb then the other on the words "here I am; here I am." Bend one thumb, then the other. Wiggle thumbs and move hands away from body. The rest of the song follows the same pattern using a different finger (both hands) each time, remembering to coordinate the actions with the words.

50 /WHERE, OH WHERE?

Words: Tom Glazer Music: Adapted by Tom Glazer (Greek)

1: Hold both arms behind back. Shake head negatively. 2: "Rock" baby in arms, then set
aside, putting arms behind back, and shake head as in verse one. 3: Repeat first verse.

ABOUT THE AUTHOR

Tom Glazer is one of the country's foremost balladeers. He started his career shortly after the great wave of "big-city" folk singing began, and performed often with Burl Ives, Leadbelly, Josh White, and others. His notable records for children include *Ballads for the Age of Science* and *On Top of Spaghetti*. He has appeared often in the theater and on leading radio and TV programs, many of which have won awards, notably his own recent show on station WQXR in New York. He is also a successful songwriter and composer, having written several hit songs and composed scores for TV and films. With Budd Schulberg he wrote songs and he composed the score for the Kazan-Schulberg, Warner Brothers film, *A Face in the Crowd*. He is the author of *A New Treasury of Folk Songs* and *Tom Glazer's Treasury of Folk Songs for the Family*.